What's Your Oil?
Unmasking Your Hidden Talents

By Maya Lynn Harris

Copyright © 2017 Maya L. Harris

Published by Redlines Publishing

Baltimore, Maryland

All rights reserved.

ISBN-13: 978-0998907215 (Redlines)

This book may not be reproduced, in whole or in part, including artwork, in any form (beyond that copying permitted by sections 107 and 108 of the U.S. Copyright law and except by reviewers for the public press), without written permission from the publisher and authors of the work.

Cover Art: "Intuition" (Adobe Stock #88284899)

Title page, headings, and body text set in Garamond

All Biblical references are from the New International Version (NIV)

Printed in the USA by Createspace, a subsidiary of Amazon.com

DEDICATION

To my sons, Bryce and Mandell,
who continue to be the reason I breathe.

To my mother, Dorothy Harris,
who taught me to fearlessly pursue my dreams.

To my father, Carl Harris,
who believed in me when no one else would.

To my brother, Jason Harris,
who makes putting pen to paper look so easy.

To my dear friend, Lorna Pinckney,
who showed me how to live love.

To the women who put their dreams on the shelf so
that others could live theirs…it's time to fly!

CONTENTS

Acknowledgments - 1

Forward - 3

The Widow - 7

The Single Mom - 9

The Non-Negotiables - 12

A Mentor's Perspective - 20

Your Most Prized Possession - 27

Know Your Network - 35

Can't Take Everyone with You - 43

A Family Affair - 48

The Possible Impossible - 53

God's Sufficiency Is Your Abundance - 58

What's Your Oil? - 62

Resources - 65

About the Author - 71

Praise for *What's Your Oil?* - 73

ACKNOWLEDGMENTS

Many thanks to my sista-mentors: Dr. Pernessa Seele, Dr. Cheryl Ivey-Green, and Yolanda Reed for seeing something in me that I was too tired to see for myself.

Thanks to my brother Jason Harris and my dear friend Cecily Gardner for editing my words so that they made sense to other people besides me.

Thanks to Jeff Marlow who boldly told me how much my original subtitle sucked! Only true friends can get away with that!

Thanks to my Reluctant Writers group for pushing me to finish. Your turn!

FOREWARD
Dr. Pernessa Seele

On any given Sunday morning, church pews across the globe are filled with people of all races, nationalities, and followers of Jesus. They are seekers of truth and righteousness and committed to following the Word of God. Yet, most of us are humble and stuck in our poverty. We have decided that to be poor is to be closer to God and to his Son, Jesus, our Lord, and Savior. Some of us can pay our bills on time, but we are humble and stuck in our lack of joy and happiness; or lack of friends and relationships. We wear our poverty like a banner of honor as Christians.

I am a believer who not only was born into a Christian family but decided to practice Christianity as an adult after exploring and studying a few world religions. With every breath, I marvel at God and His mosaic design of believers. There are many reasons for my adult decision to embrace Christianity as my life-long religious practice. Among my top 10 reasons, which I will not elaborate on, is one of the most significant: Jesus, the iconic leader of our faith, gives clear directions to his followers. *Jesus said:*

John 10:10: *"The thief does not come except to steal and to kill, and to destroy. I have come that they may have life, and have it more abundantly".*

John 14:12-14*: "Most assuredly, I say to you, he who believes in Me, the works that I do he will do also; and greater works than these he will do, because I go to my Father. And, whatever you ask in My name, that I will do, that the Father may be gloried in the Son. If you ask anything in My name, I will do it".*

I do not believe that poverty is a prerequisite for being a good Christian. I also do not embrace the prosperity teachings that suggest God will render me a car, house or one trillion dollars from the sky if I give my rent money to purchase mink coats or new cars for my pastor(s). However, I do believe in a prosperity theology that declares me a child of God, with rights to the abundant kingdom of my Father in heaven and on earth. Just like when I inherited land from my earthly father and mother, Charles & Luella Seele, I had to learn about taxes and assessments; and how to execute the role and responsibilities of land ownership and eldership in my family. I had to study to show myself approved! Throughout my adult life, I have chosen to seek new knowledge and understanding of principles that would propel my life forward that are aligned with my understanding of the teachings of Jesus.

Maya Harris, in her book, *What's Your Oil? Unmasking Your Hidden Talents* has taken the time to interlock words that provide a fresh, new view of an old tradition that has worked for many a thousand believers for generations.

These principles and strategies work. However, they only work if you work them. The impact of this book can only be witnessed in your life if you believe that the activity of work must be a part of your prayer life, and poverty (of all kind) is not a requirement to be a good Christian.

**Dr. Pernessa C. Seele,
CEO & Founder,
The Balm in Gilead, Inc.**

Maya L. Harris

THE WIDOW

II Kings 4: 1-7 (NIV)

1 The wife of a man from the company of the prophets cried out to Elisha, "Your servant my husband is dead, and you know that he revered the LORD. But now his creditor is coming to take my two boys as his slaves."

2 Elisha replied to her, "How can I help you? Tell me, what do you have in your house?"
"Your servant has nothing there at all," she said, "except a small jar of olive oil."

3 Elisha said, "Go around and ask all your neighbors for empty jars. Don't ask for just a few.

4 Then go inside and shut the door behind you and your sons. Pour oil into all the jars, and as each is filled, put it to one side."

5 She left him and shut the door behind her and her sons. They brought the jars to her and she kept pouring.

6 When all the jars were full, she said to her son, "Bring me another one." But he replied, "There is not a jar left." Then the oil stopped flowing.

7 She went and told the man of God, and he said, "Go, sell the oil and pay your debts. You and your sons can live on what is left."

THE SINGLE MOM

I was a single, broke, black mother. Don't get me wrong. I wasn't exactly a statistic – graduated high school and received a full scholarship to a Historically Black College, then graduated with my Bachelor's degree with honors. I was fully employed…with benefits. I had an apartment, a car, a 401k, and the most amazing twin sons a woman could pray for.

Still, I was a single, broke, black mother.

A few of you may wonder how that's even possible. But I would dare to guess that even more of you know EXACTLY how that's possible. I am you and you are me. Right?

How did we get here? Didn't we follow the instructions? Who can we blame?

I don't know about you. But that finger points right back to me. I was the creator of my mess. Even with an amazing support system, I consistently faced late notices, shut-off letters, and creditors' phone calls. Even when I felt like things were looking up, something ALWAYS happened to bring me back, crashing down to reality.

That is...until I met the widow.

You've read her story. The unnamed widow of II Kings. I was first introduced to her six years ago at a women's prayer breakfast. The fact that I attended this event is, in itself, a miracle. I've always been a "church girl," but did not possess the religious fervor I felt one should have in order to give up my Saturday morning in exchange for eggs, grits, and the Gospel. But there I was, enjoying the fellowship of the beautiful sisters of the church. The guest speaker that day was a college professor and minister. Breakfast was particularly good, so I missed the first few minutes of her sermon. She asked us to turn to our Bibles and open to II Kings 4: 1-7. She began to read, "The wife of a man from the company of the prophets cried out to Elisha, 'Your servant my husband is dead, and you know that he revered the LORD. But now his creditor is coming to take my two boys as his slaves.'" I looked up and around and thought, "What did she just say?" She continued to read. "Elisha replied to her, 'How can I help you? Tell me, what do you have in your house?' 'Your servant has nothing there at all,' she said, "except a small jar of olive oil.'"

What's Your Oil?

As she continued reading, my head began spinning. This sister was telling me that this single mother of two sons was completely broke, with creditors threatening her family, and she felt there was nothing she could do to stop them. In desperation, she reached out to Elisha, this man of God, widely known for his divine connections, pleading for a way out. Somehow, my life was right there, printed in the Bible!

But the widow was wrong. She did have something.

"Your servant has nothing there at all,' she said, *'except a small jar of olive oil.'"*

I learned that day, in my single/broke/black/mother mess of a life, that I had something too. And God was going to bless me just as he blessed the widow.

Now that you are reading this book, he will do the same for you. So I ask you...

What's your oil?

THE NON-NEGOTIABLES

"Your servant my husband is dead, and you know that he revered the LORD. But now his creditor is coming to take my two boys as his slaves."

The Widow

At the heart of this story, we have a mother desperate to save her sons. The widow (her name is never given) is the wife of the prophet Obadiah. Sons were very valuable to families during the widow's time. While daughters eventually moved on to their husband's family, the sons carried the family name and cared for their parents as they grew older. So, imagine this mother's crisis – not only had she lost her husband but now her sons were going to be taken away, leaving her utterly alone.

Her husband, Obadiah, a man of God, accumulated a great deal of debt from protecting and feeding the prophets who were hiding from Jezebel. Upon his death, his creditors came to collect what they were owed. You have to imagine that this mother sold everything of value in her home.

Now, the only item she owned was the pot of oil. To the widow, her sons were invaluable. She was determined to find the help she needed to save them.

゚◯゚◯゚◯゚◯

I gave birth to two amazingly perfect boys on November 11, 1996. I had already fallen in love with them during the seven months they hung out inside of me, rolling around, arguing, eating, doing backflips, and having an all-around great time at the expense of their mother's bladder and lungs. They were so excited that they decided that seven months was plenty. I could hold each of them in the palm of my hands, weighing 2 ½ and 2 pounds. The moment I laid eyes on these two little rascals, I knew that my life had forever changed and there would be nothing that I would not do for them.

Even though I was a young mother, I had several advantages. First, I was a recent college graduate with a teaching license. Finding a job would not be a difficult task once I was able to begin searching. Second, since I attended Virginia Union University on a full scholarship, I did not have any student loans to worry about. I did have one credit card that I managed to max out my junior year and a gym bill that I neglected. But things could have been worse. Third, and most importantly, I had an amazing support system. My parents welcomed me back with open arms and looked forward to having two, little faces brightening up their home. I made a commitment to put money away and limit my time there; I did not want to be a burden on them. So, I had it made. Minimal debt, no rent, and minor bills. But...

Someone forgot to tell me how much hospital stays cost.

My sons were born prematurely and had to remain in the hospital for seven weeks in the NICU. I was still covered under my father's insurance, but my sons were not. I had no income and no job since I was ordered to stay on bed rest during the final six weeks of my pregnancy. I was hesitant to get any government assistance but finally opted to get insurance for the boys and WIC. I knew that I would be able to work fairly soon, so I did not apply for income assistance nor food stamps. Instead, I applied for two credit cards for emergencies and began looking for part-time work as soon as I could. While my finances were low, I managed with the help of my parents and good friends.

I took on a few part-time jobs once the boys were discharged from the hospital and were gaining weight steadily. I eventually got my first teaching position and moved out of my parents' home to our first apartment.

Without the safety net that my family provided, I soon realized the true expense of having twins as a single mother. Since I was not receiving any financial support from their father at the time, I struggled on my salary, buying double of everything! Credit card debt began to rack up, and even with occasional help from my parents, I sunk further and further into a money pit. I knew that I had to make some changes. I moved back home for one year, saved all I could, and eventually moved to Virginia with a new job, car, apartment, and money in the bank.

Initially, things began to look up after the move. While I was making less money, my expenses were much lower and my sons' father stepped up and began to help out. But the cost of daycare and other expenses began to creep up on me. Since I was never a great money manager, I started to incur expenses that became disasters: store credit cards, new, higher car payments once my first car died, payday loans to take care of high utility bills, and more. I was digging a hole in quicksand and had no way of getting out. Every step forward became a step back. I took on extra responsibilities at work, which brought in more income, but required more childcare. I went back to school to get my master's degree, which led to a raise but added the burden of student loans and higher taxes. I was spending less time with my sons and more time doing the things that I liked the least. After having to stay with a friend for two weeks when our lights were shut off, I had reached the end of my rope. My children were sleeping on someone's couch because I had financially lost control. I knew the widow's pain even before I knew her story. Something had to give.

I began to push. To hustle. To make better decisions. To ask for professional financial help.

Getting advice to begin a business was the first step to my financial breakthrough. I had a long road ahead, but I had two little people watching me. I would never, ever give up. I owed them the world.

※※※※※

My story is not a drastic as the widow's story. No one was going to take my children away. But their well-being was at stake. The two people who I hold most dear to me were suffering due to situations both out of my control and due to lack of my control. We were not living the life that we were meant to live. I had reached a point of desperation that I never wanted to allow my children to experience again. I was not willing to negotiate their future due to my present circumstances.

What are your non-negotiables? Where do you draw the line? At what point have you said, "Enough is enough. I will not allow this to happen anymore." Recognizing what or who your non-negotiables are will allow you to frame all of your future decisions. This journey will definitely require some sacrifice. But once you know WHO you are doing this for, you will always have the wind of motivation at your back, pushing you forward to greatness.

Write It Out

What or who exactly is your NON-NEGOTIABLE? Your NON-NEGOTIABLE (or your "WHY") is whatever or whoever is so important to you that you'd do anything to protect it and nurture it. A mentor once told me, "If your WHY doesn't make you cry, then it's not big enough." Your "why" totally depends on you! For me, it's my children. I'm willing to sacrifice anything for their well-being. For many people, their NON-NEGOTIABLE is a family member or members or even a unique idea, goal, or lifestyle (ex: a monk who sacrifices anything for his faith).

Your NON-NEGOTIABLE is up to you. But I CAN tell you what it is not. Your NON-NEGOTIABLE isn't money. Some of the unhappiest people in the world are the richest people. It has to be bigger than money. It has to have a lasting impact. It has to make you whole.

Think about it. Muse over it. Then, write about your NON-NEGOTIABLES. It will be your main source of motivation through this journey.

My Non-Negotiables

What's Your Oil?

A MENTOR'S PERSPECTIVE

2 Elisha replied to her, "How can I help you..."

The Widow

Elisha was the successor of the prophet Elijah. He continued Elijah's work against the ruling dynasty of Omri, overthrowing King Ahab and replacing him with Jehu. Elisha was no doubt familiar with Obadiah's great faith and recognized the importance of assisting his widow, particularly since Mosaic law insisted that widows and fatherless children be cared for.

However, it is more even more important to recognize that the widow reached out to Elisha for help. Despite all of her efforts, she was unable to solve her problem on her own. Since we know that she and her husband were people of great faith, we have to assume that there were many prayers lifted during this time of turmoil. Yet, the widow recognized that it was time to ask for help. She did not give up on prayer; in fact, it is just the opposite.

What's Your Oil?

The widow saw Elisha's arrival as an answer to her prayers! She confidently reached out to someone who she knew had the kind of the relationship with God that He could work through Elisha during her time of greatest need.

※※※※※※

You can't take everyone's advice. That was a lesson I learned at a very young age. My mother used to say to me, "Everyone who smiles in your face ain't necessarily your friend, Maya." But of course, like most stubborn teenagers, I had to find that out for myself. Over the years, I learned to trust His voice in guiding me, like the widow, to the individuals who could, and eventually would, become mentors who changed my life.

As an English teacher, I frequently helped friends with editing their work. Books, reports, college papers, poems -- I would gladly lend a hand with my keen eye for errors and inconsistencies. One day, Rev. Dr. Cheryl Ivey-Green, the assistant pastor at my church, a woman I had grown to admire a great deal, approached me about helping her with the final edits of her doctoral dissertation. Her editor was unable to complete the project and she needed someone for "clean-up" editing. Of course, I agreed. I had never worked on a dissertation before. In fact, I had no desire to write one of my own. But I took the time to study the requirements, review the format, and complete the work she needed. After the acceptance of her work, she happily offered to recommend me to her classmates. She said to me, "Maya, you should do this! People are always looking for good editors." She was very aware of my financial struggles and she knew the idea of starting an editing business would be very attractive to me. I never considered being an editor. I was just something I did as a favor. Besides, why would anyone seek me out as an editor? Despite my self-doubt, her advice lingered with me for months and proved to be some of the most valuable advice I had ever been given. But I'll tell you more about that later!

I met my second mentor at the New Members class when I first joined the church. She was (and is) a church deacon and taught the first class that I had to take when my sons and I joined the church. My first class was a scene right out of a reality TV show. At that time, I was dating a brother who decided that he would join the church as well and attended class with me. Little did I know that his ex-wife was also in the class (who had no problem telling the class who she was)! Completely horrified and embarrassed, I prayed the class would just end as quickly as possible. But Deacon Yolanda Reed took the situation and taught from it, sharing her own story of marriage and divorce with us. After class, she approached me, asked if I was OK, and offered her help in any way she could. From that day on, she always checked on me and advised me. One year, she gave me an opportunity to earn some extra money by working in her office. Not only was she a deacon, but she is also the CEO of a very successful credentialing firm. At that time, she knew I was at the beginning of starting my own entrepreneurial journey and consistently offered advice. One day, she sat down with me as I shared a new idea I was developing. She told me, "Maya, when I see you, you are covered in gold. You have no idea of the wealth inside of you. But something is blocking you. You are wearing your pain. You must deal with whatever it is that is stopping you. When you do, money will never be an issue for you again. Your blessing will be a blessing to others. So, figure it out and do something about it." She was right. I was getting in the way of my own success. If she never helped me again (which she did and continues to do) those words would have been enough. That was a lesson I needed to learn. It was time to act.

My third angel was by far the most unexpected. I met her at the same church. She did not attend church regularly. In fact, I only saw her a few times per year when she would come to address the congregation about the National Week of Prayer for the Healing of Aids. Dr. Pernessa Seele is an internationally recognized activist and a powerful woman of God. I was amazed that she was a member of our church! But my respect for her does not just stem from the work she has done around the world. I have been able to get to know her on a personal level after she asked me to edit the program for a conference she sponsored each year, at the recommendation from Rev. Cheryl and Yolanda. I was thrilled at the opportunity. That editing assignment then turned into an invitation to join the conference team as an on-site writer and show script caller. I found myself in the company of internationally recognized faith leaders, doctors, scientists, and gospel artists. More importantly, I was surrounded by professionals that came together every year to make the conference a success. Event planners, public relation specialists, engineers, and more were the experts on the team. And here I was, this amateur editor/English teacher taking it all in. Dr. Seele sat and spoke with me toward the end of the event. Over a glass of wine, I told her how the event gave me unexpected clarity and motivation. I asked her, "Dr. Seele, I'm curious. Why me?" She replied, "You have no idea how good you are. You are smart, talented, and creative, but you're all over the place. What do you really want? What do you really want to do? When you figure that out, you'll be unstoppable. We'll all be attending *your* events." Once again, I had been exposed. I was blocking my own blessing. I had to figure WHAT I wanted. I had listened to what HE had placed in my heart and follow the path He was creating for me.

People come into your life for many reasons. Some are there to teach you a lesson. Some will come to guide you through a certain time in your life. Some are there to take the journey with you. He will always send you what you need. While there have been many wonderful people in my life, I am forever grateful to my three angels who gave me clarity, tough love, and guidance when I needed it most. Over the years, I have had other mentors for different reasons and additional journeys. I am grateful that I was obedient and listened to those he sent my way.

If you pay attention, you will begin to recognize the people that have been sent you as your guides on your journey. But how do you know when someone is a mentor versus someone who just has good advice? From my experience, a good mentor has five important qualities:

1. Compassionate - Good mentors will genuinely care about your well-being and your success. While they may not always say what you want to hear, they will always keep your feelings in mind when sharing their advice.

2. Honest – Your mentor will never be your "Yes Man." She or he will care too much about you to just tell you things to make you feel good. While tactful, the honest mentor will always help you see things as they really are.

3. Objective – it is important that you see things from all sides. A good mentor will help you analyze all sides of an issue – areas that will both benefit and not benefit you. However, they will allow you to make your own decisions.

4. Curious – Questions! Your mentor should have all kinds of questions for you. Questions about your life, your goals, your fears, your dreams and more. She or he will realize that your experiences will help shape your future, so she or he will seek to understand the complete you.

5. Approachable – Your mentor can not make you feel inferior or foolish. She or he is open, understanding, and patient. In fact, your mentor will recognize that they were once in your shoes and can

empathize with your current position.

Having the right mentor is an important part of your entrepreneurial journey. Find someone who fits these qualities and be unafraid, like the widow, to ask for help and guidance when you need it most!

Write It Out

Your mentor may be someone you already know or someone you may only know of. As you are considering possible mentors, think of those who fit the qualities I listed and have successful experience in the area in which you re seeking help. List them, compare their qualities, and decide on who you will approach for assistance.

My Potential Mentors

Names	Qualities

YOUR MOST PRIZED POSSESSION

2 Elisha replied to her, "How can I help you? Tell me, what do you have in your house?"
"Your servant has nothing there at all," she said, "except a small jar of olive oil."

The Widow

Realizing that she had run out of options, the widow reached out to Elisha. Elisha had a divine connection that she felt was powerful than her own. One can imagine, as a believer, she already prayed. Relentlessly. She sought the answers for herself but now felt that her efforts weren't enough. So, you can imagine the moment of panic that she must have experienced when Elisha asked her, "Tell me, what do you have in your house?" The frustration surely began to rise within her! The creditors were on their way to take her children from her! Obviously, there was nothing of any value that could possibly matter…

…"except a small jar of olive oil."

Something so insignificant. She overlooked it because, on the surface, it had no value. It was so small she couldn't even sell it (or it would have been long gone). One can almost sense a hint of sarcasm in her statement, almost a dare.

But isn't that like God? To take something that we overlook as worthless and make a miracle from it? In my English classes, I would stop at this point in the story to define dramatic irony, a point in a story when the reader knows more than the characters. As readers, we know what God can do with that oil! We saw him do it with fish and bread. We've seen him do it in our own lives. The widow did not realize it at the time, but that small, insignificant jar of oil, her only possession, the jar no one else wanted, was going to be the tool that God used to work a miracle in her life.

※※※※※

At the women's conference prayer breakfast, the speaker got to this point in the story and began preaching from it. I'm embarrassed to say that I had stopped paying attention. Sitting at the table, slightly hyperventilating, I was overcome by the story. I had to have reread that verse ten times.

"…except a small jar of olive oil."

I began to write in my notebook.

What's my oil?
What's my oil?
What's my oil?

What did I have that I took for granted? What did I possess that no one else wanted? What was mine whether I felt I wanted it or not? I started brainstorming (as any good English teacher would). I didn't outright own anything. I was a renter. I was barely paying my car note. I did not own any property, jewelry, stock, nor bonds. I owned clothes and furniture. Was that my oil? I suppose I could sell stuff online. I could go through my closet and bring clothes to a consignment shop. But I knew that would not solve anything. I was broke and behind on every bill. I didn't need a bit of cash. I needed a miracle. Then I recalled the times that I climbed my soapbox in my classroom and told my students that their education was invaluable. No matter what happens, it can never be taken from you. I started listening to my own sermon. My education. My six-year, B.A./M.S. education could never be taken away from me. So, I wrote that down.

My education.

But that felt too broad. Yet, I realized that I was on the right path because my face began to feel flushed. I looked around the room and caught a glimpse of Rev. Cheryl. Rev. Cheryl is the mentor I mentioned earlier whose dissertation I edited. The moment I looked at her, I thought to myself, "Well, you definitely know how to edit. No one wants to do that. So, I scribbled it in my notebook.

Editor

I stared at the page for, what seemed like, an eternity. I circled it.

And then I cried. I felt a small chill run down my back. I got a bit dizzy and cried some more. By that time, the room was standing and clapping and praising the Lord. The speaker was phenomenal, and everyone seemed to have felt the spirit in the room. However, I knew that God had not sent me to the breakfast to hear her entire sermon. He closed my ears and made me listen to the words he was writing in my heart. I had found my oil.

(Finishing my praise dance)

That moment was such a gift. It still makes me shiver just thinking about how powerful it was to come to the realization that God had already given me everything I needed – I just needed to sit still long enough to listen. Isn't that the hardest part? Sitting still? Our days are filled with so many responsibilities, some that were given to us and some that we took on ourselves. Every hour seems to be spent long before it happens. The stress that is created as a result leads us down a dark path toward depression, anxiety, obesity, and more. We spend less time with family.

What's Your Oil?

We spend less time doing the things we love. We forget about the dreams we once had as children. Life simply gets in the way.

Yet, that isn't what He wants for any of us. This beautiful planet was not created for us to ignore. We were not given decades to live, just to spend each day miserable. Do you realize that you are here for a reason? We could have easily been given the same life span as a dog or even a housefly. No, we were given 70, 80, 90 + years on this planet to make an impact. You can't do that with your head down, dragging your way through the week. He gave you a purpose and is doing everything He can to direct you toward it.

But you must be willing to listen.

There's something that you love doing. Something that you would do even if no one paid you to do it. Something that makes you feel alive. Something that no one can take from you. It's yours. Maybe you have a knack for cooking. Or maybe you were voted "Most likely to star in a Broadway Play" in high school. Are you the person who lives for waking up on a Saturday and cleaning your house? Can you nurse dead plants back to life? Do you have a keen eye for fashion? Or maybe you are like me and can spot a typo 30 feet away. Whatever it is, we all have that something inside of us.

The problem is, at some point, someone told you that your dream was silly. Someone who never followed his/her own path stopped you from going down yours. Someone told you that you had to get ready for the "real world" and your silly, little gift would not pay the bills. So, you listened. You did the "right" thing. You may even have found immense success in taking that advice. Yet, there is a part of you that feels empty and incomplete. You begin searching for answers everywhere. I know! I did it too! You are searching outside of yourself because the thing that brings you so much joy and peace seems too insignificant for your "real world" problems.

"...except a small jar of olive oil."

The widow did not realize her blessing was in front of her all along. So is yours. The one thing that will bring you fulfillment, leave an impact on the world, and save your life is already in your possession. It may be raw, untrained, a bit broken and dirty. But it is there. Waiting for you to remember how it makes you feel. All you have to do is sit and listen long enough for it to tell you how to find it again.

Write It Out

Spend some time brainstorming ideas. Write down things that you love doing, used to love doing, and is or was really good at doing! Don't edit yourself. Reach back into the sandbox and work your way up to today. Somewhere on that list, your oil will appear!

What's My Oil?

Maya L. Harris

KNOW YOUR NETWORK

"3 Elisha said, "Go around and ask all your neighbors for empty jars. Don't ask for just a few."

The Widow

There are many scriptures in the Bible that focus on hospitality and how to treat your neighbors. During this time, it was customary to welcome your neighbors, even traveling strangers, into your home to provide food, shelter, and entertainment. Elisha instructed the widow to go to all her neighbors and ask for empty jars. She and her sons were to ask for as many as possible.

While this may be considered soliciting today, the widow's neighbors would not dare deny her of this request. It would have been considered improper. She was able to gather many jars to bring to her home.

The widow also had to be comfortable enough to

carry out the task. Remember, she was at the end of her rope and had already lost everything. This had to be a humbling experience for her! With her position in the community, going from being the wife of a priest to going door-to-door asking all of her neighbors for help had to be tremendously difficult. However, she knew her neighbors and their traditions well enough that the task was easily done.

I hate asking for help.

I'm the baby of the family on both my mother's and father's sides. The youngest grandchild. Admittedly a bit spoiled, I always felt like everyone took care of me, whether I wanted it or not. I always felt like "the baby." Even as a woman with children of my own, I had a tough time being accepted as an adult. When my finances began to strain, I would try every avenue to hustle money before breaking down to reach out. I was embarrassed that I still needed my parents' support as a parent myself. In my attempts to "pull myself up by my bootstraps" I fell further and further behind. When I did finally break down, it was because daycare fees were due or the lights and/or water had been turned off. I tried to start many little side hustles to avoid asking help. I took on extra responsibilities at school, joined several network marketing companies (some great, some not), and more. I felt like the widow – at the end of my rope, barely hanging on.

When this idea of starting my own editing/writing company was placed in me, I was elated! This was something that not only I could do with my eyes closed (seriously, I can smell a comma splice), but it had already proven to be financially rewarding. It did not require any significant start-up costs, just some planning, and marketing.

Marketing. Great. How do I do that?

Social media will give a new entrepreneur the impression that if you post it, they will come. All you have to do is make a cool flyer and post it on your Facebook page and the customers will come knocking on your door.

Naw. That ain't it.

I quickly learned that in order to build my business, I would have to do more than create a clever meme. I would need to develop a plan! As a network marketer, one lesson I learned was the power of your "warm market" – family, friends, and colleagues. While these groups of the people closest to you may not become your customers (in fact, most won't), they are often your biggest cheerleaders and willing to spread the word about your new venture. Everyone you know knows hundreds of people that you don't know. Many times, new business owners fall into the trap of trying to make their warm market their only customers. They are, in fact, gateways to your potential customer base.

So, I made a list of people I was closest to that

may be able to connect me to potential clients. My future customers would need editing help. I thought of my friends, family, and co-workers that knew authors, college students, poets, and business owners. In fact, it was a cousin that gave me the idea of adding resumes to my services. Each person on my list willing gave me names and advice because I did not ask for money. They saw that I was doing something for myself and they happily supported me. Since I knew and understood my network, I understood how to approach them this time. And they blessed me in return.

※※※※※※※

Let's take some time to evaluate your network by focusing on those who are closest to you – your family and friends.

I need to start this off by saying that your family and friends can be your greatest supporters. But they can also be your greatest obstacles. Understand that they mean well. But most of us grew up learning that success meant going to school and getting a good job with benefits. Very few families encouraged their children to start a business. I'm sure some did, but not many. The idea of owning a business for most people is scary. There's too much uncertainty. Too many risks. Don't be surprised if you hear things like…

"You're starting a business? Did you lose your job?"
"What kind of hustle are you running now?"

"What do you know about running a business. Don't burn any bridges!"
"You need to go out there and go get a real job."

Our family and friends say things like this because they are aware of the high failure rate of new businesses. They aren't wrong for worrying. But any dream worth having is worth fighting for! Starting a business is just as tough as starting a new job, tougher in fact. But just like a new job, you get the proper training, make some mistakes, and grow.

A mentor once told me that it is important to seek support from family and friends so that you get used to hearing the word "no" early! As funny as this may seem, there's a great deal of truth to it. However, there's a way to get support from your family without asking for support.

Look at your family and friends as a connection to a much larger network. Your future clients are beyond the limits of who you already know. While those closest to you may not be able to support you financially, they may be willing to connect you to others who have resources that you need. You just need to ask the right questions.

Step 1 – Make a list of the 25 people closest to you. Family, friends, co-workers, church members, etc. These are the people you invite your wedding or birthday party. The folks you send Christmas cards to and vacation with. Write down their names and contact information so that you have it in front of you.

Step 2 – Write down your relationship with them. How do you know each of these people and for how long?

Step 3 – What unique quality and skill do they have that may benefit you on your business journey? Do they have a large network? Are they active in the community? Are they influencers? Do they own a truck? Do they have a connection to someone in banking? Think of anything that might assist you later on.

Step 4 – Start talking! Begin making your calls. Let each person know that you are starting a business. Be clear that you are NOT asking for money, just some direction. Ask them to help in the way that you know they are able to. But avoid asking for cash! Why? We all get bombarded with people asking for money. Most of us are willing to help folks who seem to be helping themselves. This does not mean that you won't eventually need support (maybe through crowd-funding). But they will be more willing to support you later once they've seen how serious you are now. Remember, the widow did not ask for money from her neighbors. She asked for empty jars. This was much easier request that blessed her in the end.

Step 5 – Follow up with a "Thank You!" This will go a long way. Calling your Aunt Cathy to thank her for connecting you to her designer who helped you make the perfect flyer (who also spoke so highly of her) will help build trust that you are serious about your business. When you call Aunt Cathy back because you need to raise $2000 for some additional supplies, Aunt Cathy will be more likely to support you. She may even become your first customer because she now feels like she contributed to your success.

Your family and friends want to see you succeed. Why? Because if you can, then so can they! Just understand who they each are and how to approach them and they will gladly "share their jars" with you!

Write It Out

Make a list of 25 people: family and friends that you are in contact with regularly.

Name	How do you know me?	Contact Info
1.		
2.		
3.		
4.		
5.		
6.		
7.		
8.		
9.		
10.		
11.		
12.		
13.		
14.		
15.		
16.		
17.		
18.		
19.		
20.		
21.		
22.		
23.		
24.		
25.		

CAN'T TAKE EVERYONE WITH YOU

"4 Then go inside and shut the door behind you and your sons...5 She left him and shut the door behind her and her sons."

The Widow

Elisha instructed the widow, along with her sons, to go out to all their neighbors and gather as many jars as possible. So, the three of them, door to door, went into their neighborhood to seek assistance. As the tradition dictates, the neighbors gladly assisted. However, it is certain that the widow had to give some type of explanation to the neighbors. It is also certain that the neighbors knew her situation. Her husband was a prominent member of the community, so his death and the resulting calamities that had fallen upon his wife and children had to have been widely known...and discussed.

This may have been thousands of years ago, but human nature has not changed. Even then, people gossiped about one another. It may not have to have malicious intent, but people talk. And when people talk, they also tend to want to give advice. I'm sure the widow received a great deal of "what you should do" suggestions as she went door to door. There were probably people who even offered to help bring the jars to her home. She was, after all, the wife of Obadiah. It would only be right to help her and her sons with this odd request and possibly get a glimpse of what she planned on doing with all those jars.

But Elisha's instructions were very clear, "...then go inside and shut the door behind you and your sons." He did not tell her to let people bring the jars inside. What was to happen for this family was a blessing that was explicitly for them. Some of the greatest blessings in the Bible happened behind closed doors. Moses witnessed the Burning Bush alone. Jesus raised the child from her deathbed only after instructing her family to close the door and keep the mourners outside. He gave sight to the blind man away from the crowds. There are times that we will only receive our blessings once we walk away from the eyes and ears of the people around us and find ourselves alone with the Lord, free from distraction.

༺༻༺༻༺༻

I've worked with some of the best people on the planet. In my earliest business ventures, the first thing I would do is to seek out someone else who could help me build my dream. I'll say that again -- the first thing I would do is seek out *someone else* who could help *me* build *my* dream.

And that was my downfall in partnerships. I had a very specific vision for what I wanted to see my new company do. But since I did not trust my own gifts, I would immediately look for someone else who would partner with me. However, when you take on a partner, you must be willing to recognize their vision as well. This is different than building a team to run your business. A partner has an equal stake in the vision, mission, and goals of your business. Even when I knew the Lord had placed a particular purpose in my heart, I did not trust myself enough to carry out His will. So, roadblocks would appear. God was trying to get my attention. When I started my latest company, LAMA Learning, I finally recognized that in order to fulfill the purpose He had placed in me, I would have to trust him enough to "shut the door" and allow him to speak through me. It was not until I stepped back and let him guide me that I saw what he wanted me to do. I was able to build the company that I envisioned that then opened the door to hiring the right team, finding the right mentor, securing the right resources, and developing a strong plan.

God's blessing for me will bless everyone around me, but I had to give Him that private time to bless me with what was intended just for me.

As you begin your entrepreneurial journey, you are going to encounter many types of people. You always have supporters – individuals that have your back no matter what. They are your cheering section and will gladly come to your aid when called. Then you meet your "well-wishers". These folks may initially seem like supporters, but manage to say things like, "Weeelll, I wish you would take some time to think this through more." They mean well, but will quickly zap your energy. Of course, you will have "haters." However, I rarely acknowledge them because there's no need to allow any negative energy to be a part of your story. So that's enough talk about them.

As you work on planting, nurturing, growing, and harvesting your idea, pay close attention to who is a part of the planning process. For the widow, her sons played an integral role in God's plan for her. Be sure to ask Him for guidance on who should be in your inner circle. This is a place of trust and full commitment. It is not for everyone. Share your plans and ideas with people who can actually help it grow. This is not the time for cheerleaders; this is a time for your strongest players. Know what everyone brings to the table. Don't allow your personal feelings about someone influence their role in this process. You must protect it as you would your child. Your dream is depending on you!

What's Your Oil?

Write It Out

Using the chart below, write down the individuals you plan on working closely with during the planning stages. It's OK if you don't know everyone's role yet. Nor do you have to fill out each space. Your inner circle is determined by you!

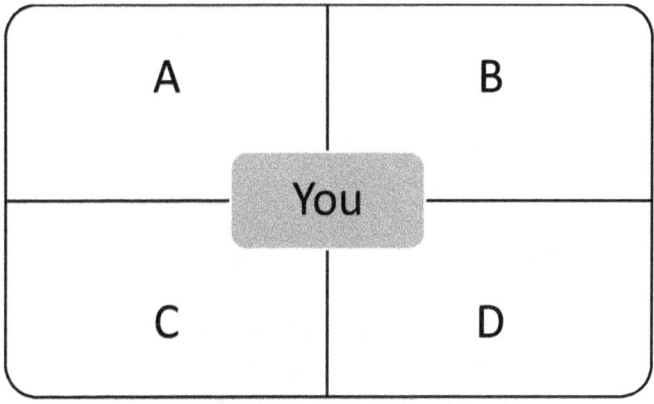

A FAMILY AFFAIR

5 She left him and shut the door behind her and her sons. They brought the jars to her and she kept pouring

The Widow

Elisha instructed the widow to work with her sons to gather the jars and shut the door behind them. No one was would witness the miracle that was about to take place. As with the miracle mentioned in the previous chapter, some blessings are just meant for your eyes only. Yet, Elisha did not leave her sons outside. They became an integral part of the blessing. As sons, heirs of their father's legacy, financially, there was nothing left for them to inherit. Everything had been sold just to keep the family alive. All that they had left was their mother and their father's name.

Despite not having the worldly inheritance, the sons of Obadiah were left with much more – a blessing from God. Not only a blessing, but the unique opportunity to see the blessing happen, alongside their mother. After experiencing the pain of losing their father and everything they own, watching their mother struggle and suffer day after day, and fearing for their own safety, these sons received a gift far greater than any inheritance. Behind closed doors, this family came face-to-face with God. For that, their lives had been changed forever.

※※※※※

I remember the first time that I got to hold my sons. It wasn't the moment they were born, like most. They were premature and too small to hold. Upon birth, I got a brief look at them and they were rushed to the NICU. It wasn't until the next day that I had a chance to head down to see them in their little incubators. Mandell, who is three minutes older than his brother, was just over three pounds. Bryce, his feisty twin, weighed in just over two pounds. I remember holding their tiny hands in mine and being overwhelmed with a sense of awe. These two mini-men were here and needed me more than anyone ever had. I held them for the first time ten days later. One in each arm, each wearing giant nursery caps that the hospital volunteers had knitted for them. They were too small for newborn clothes, so they wore doll clothes for the first few weeks. They even had to wear doll diapers! Here they were, my perfect twins, ready and waiting for their momma to guide them through life.

Fast forward 15 years. Mandell and Bryce had grown up to be just as amazing as I had dreamed. Intelligent, kind, talented, funny, and ready to take on the world. Despite our struggles over the years, they continued to be my biggest cheerleaders. When I decided to start the editing company, Bryce said, "That makes sense, Mom. You do that all day anyway. Might as well get paid for it." They passed out flyers, helped me set up my office, and did odd jobs (with a bit of grumbling) when I needed them to. While they were not quite old enough to help me with the actual work, they did what they could to support me, even if it meant cooking dinner while I worked in my office. That was blessing enough.

Throughout the entire planning, growing, and building process, I made it a point to be very transparent with them. I wanted them to understand why I decided to start a business, what it meant for our future, and how they could help. As a single mom, I did not have the luxury of having a spouse that could support me when things became difficult. So, the boys became my sounding board, my idea consultants, and my critics. They truly inspired me to stay focused on my goals.

༺༻༺༻༺༻

Your family can play a key role in your success. While the twins gave me the support I needed from home, I also was blessed to have my parents and my brother behind me 100%. However, I realized that Mandell and Bryce were the motivation I needed to push past the pain. They continue to inspire me and make me a better person every day.

Whether it is your children, parents, spouse, siblings, or someone you consider to be family, your blessing may include someone closest to you who has experienced difficulties with you. While the journey to run a business may be a difficult one, you don't have to go through it alone. Whether you have a partner or a sounding board, God will put someone in your corner to walk this journey with you. Together, you too will have the opportunity to witness God's power to work miracles in your life!

Write It Out

Take a moment to reflect on the individuals who have supported you in your life and helped carried you through your challenges. How would it bless you to have them a part of your business journey? How would it bless them?

THE POSSIBLE IMPOSSIBLE

4 Then go inside and shut the door behind you and your sons. Pour oil into all the jars, and as each is filled, put it to one side."
5 She left him and shut the door behind her and her sons. They brought the jars to her and she kept pouring.

The Widow

The widow did everything that the prophet Elisha has asked her to do. She and her sons went out into the community and borrowed all of the jars that they could. They shut themselves behind closed doors and awaited further instructions from Elisha. Elisha instructed them to begin pouring oil from their small jar into the larger jars. Without question and without hesitation, the widow began to pour the oil into the jars. From a few drops came gallons and gallons of oil until each jar had been filled!

Not at any point, did the widow ask, "How was

that supposed to work? How am I supposed to fill all of these jugs with such a small amount of oil?" The widow's faith in God and her belief that Elisha was connected to God allowed her to receive a blessing that many people would not be open to receive. It was her faith in God and Elisha's words that filled the jars. Just as the jars, we are empty vessels that God is willing to fill with his blessings once we are open to receive it.

※※※※※※

I never edited a doctoral dissertation until Rev. Cheryl Ivy-Green asked me to complete hers. I've never run a business on my own until I began editing. I thought about it before and definitely had several attempts at small, side "hustles", but never had I obtained in EIN and put my name on a business application. I simply did not think that I had the training, time, resources, nor talent to run a business. I quickly learned, once I got out of my own way and handing things over to God, he instilled in me all of the areas that I felt I lacked in. He opened the doors that not only were closed but weren't even there to begin with. However, none of this would have happened if I hadn't sat still long enough to listen to what he was trying to teach me. Those quiet words at the women's prayer breakfast that morning touched me in a way that nothing else had before.

I spent hours studying my craft. Then, I spent more hours studying business. I attended seminars, began following business icons, and asking a lot of questions. I learned to take advantage of local resources. I began studying Tony Robbins, Eric Thomas, and Les Brown to learn how to capture an audience and hone my message. I learned to network with other business owners and forged relationships that I still value to this day. I recognized that the blessing given to me was not a magic wand, but a key. He blessed me with the tools to accomplish my dreams, not the dream itself. Just like the widow, I had to do my part to make the impossible possible for my family. For, "Faith without works is dead," (James 2:17) so I knew that I must put in the effort to prove my worthiness of the blessing he had shown me.

※※※※※

There is nothing too hard for God. All your hopes and dreams are but a blink of an eye for Him. Your self-doubt reflects your lack of faith in Him. It is time to quiet your fears and trust that He has a blessing that is meant just for you. But you must ask. What is it that you dream of doing that you have been too afraid to try? What talent or skill have you been neglecting because someone once told you to let go of your "silly" dreams get yourself a "real" job? What blessing are you denying simply because you are afraid? God knows your needs and still ready and willing to bless you with all the tools to accomplish anything.

It is time to stop wishing and pray for that which is already marked as yours!

Write It Out

Take a moment to write out a prayer, asking God to bless you with the tools you need to accomplish your dreams. Be specific! This is not the time to speak in generalities and assume He will translate it for you. Write it down and make it plain! Your blessing is on its way!

What's Your Oil?

GOD'S SUFFICIENCY IS YOUR ABUNDANCE

6 When all the jars were full, she said to her son, "Bring me another one." But he replied, "There is not a jar left." Then the oil stopped flowing.
7 She went and told the man of God, and he said, "Go, sell the oil and pay your debts. You and your sons can live on what is left."

The Widow

As the widow poured what seemed like an endless flow of oil from the jar, her sons continued to bring more and more jugs that had been collected from their neighbors. Jug after jug was filled to the rim. The moment that the last jug was filled the oil stopped.

Elisha gave the widow and her sons instructions to go back and sell the oil to her neighbors. The sale of the oil would not only pay all of her debts but allow her and her sons to live comfortably for the rest of their lives. As the reader, one has to remember that once the widow sold all of their belongings, she also depleted any reserves that would have become her sons' inheritance. It was her goal to save her children's lives and keep them from a life of slavery. And what was God's response? Abundance for her and her children! He rewarded her faith with more than she could have ever prayed for.

Imagine the "buzz" that would be created in the neighborhood when the family returned with overflowing jars of oil to sell! The cheers and the jeers that the widow must have encountered. However, for those who understood the power of prayer, this blessing would not come as a surprise. The entire community received a blessing simply due to the widow's faith. That's how God's love works. Not only will he bless you, but your blessing will become a blessing to others.

Initially, I did very little advertising. I didn't really need to. The majority of my clients came to me through word of mouth. One dissertation led to another. One resume led to another. One book led to another. Once I realized that I had a knack for business, I invested more into my training and marketing. I helped other business owners get started. I developed additional income streams. I tried, I failed, I tried again. Every moment has been a learning experience. Yet, I never lost sight of why I was able to do what I loved. HE blessed me with all of the tools I would ever need to be successful. Ephesians 6:10-18 teaches us about the Armor of God. I feel even more blessed with some additional tools:

Maya's Divine Armor:
- Helmet of Knowledge – I did not realize that the education I received would prepare me for this journey. I thought I'd always be a teacher. But He saw fit guide me towards learning skills outside of the classroom that would shape my entrepreneurial path. Everything from having a talent with presenting to a gift with computers, my unique skill set has made and saved me money along the way!
- Sword of Persistence – I never give up. I get knocked down, laughed at and scorned, but I get back up every time. This tool has allowed me to not be afraid to give another "stab" at it! (Pardon the pun)
- Shield of Discernment – God truly blessed me with my "Spidey Sense". While there are amazing coaches, partners, and opportunities out there for entrepreneurs, there are an equal amount of charlatans and thieves. As my mom would say, "I can smell 'em a mile away!"
- Heart of Compassion – I know. The heart isn't a weapon, but any soldier fighting for what she believes in needs to have it. I truly love what I do and I love the people I can help. I am driven to make this world a better place. I don't need millions of dollars to measure my success. I just want someone that can say, "You've changed my life." With that, my cup runneth over.

Write It Out

His blessing to you will be enough. It will be more than you can ever imagine. But first, you must recognize how he is blessing you. He is not a God that just blesses you with material things. His greatest gift is the blessing of the tools that allow us to do for ourselves. Use the terms below to describe the tools He has blessed you with!

Your Divine Armor:
- Helmet of _____ :

_____
_____
_____
_____

- Sword of _____ :

_____
_____
_____
_____

- Shield of _____ :

_____
_____
_____
_____

- Heart of _____ :

_____
_____
_____
_____

WHAT'S YOUR OIL?

In 2011, I attended a prayer breakfast that ultimately changed the course of my life. I remember sitting there, stressing over bills and money and the basics my kids and I would need to survive. As much as I wanted to focus in on the music in the fellowship, my life was crashing down all around me and I just didn't know what to do. He found me that day in the prayer breakfast. He knew exactly what I needed to be able to hear him. I mean really hear him. He didn't send me a vague sign. He sent me a story about me. The widow and I had so much in common, there was no way for me to even be able to ignore her story. I think about all the years I spent in Sunday School and church listening to a sermon after sermon and I don't have any recollection of hearing the story of the widow. I'm sure someone spoke on it before. But it wasn't until that day did I actually meet her.

It's now 2017. I am no longer a classroom teacher. I was able to take a leap of faith 4 years ago and leave my job. I walked away from my place of comfort. I ran my editing firm and a few other ventures until the opportunity to become an independent educational consultant was given to me. I jumped at the chance to be in the classroom again, only this time having a direct impact on the educators working with the children. It was this move that led me to open my educational service company, LAMA Learning (Language Arts & Math Associates). While the road hasn't been easy, I've been blessed to be given more than one jar of oil. And they all are working together. My dreams are coming true every day, right in front of me.

My sons, now 20 years old, have their own entrepreneurial goals. Remember, they do as we do, not as we say. Mandell has his associate's degree in culinary arts and is going to finish his bachelor's in business management so that he can open up his own catering business. Bryce is pursuing his degree in sound engineering so that he can open up his own music studio. My lessons helped instill lessons in them. They recognize that it was okay to live out their dreams and to tap into their talents. I remember one day Bryce was considering becoming a history teacher because he thought that that's what I would want him to do. We sat and had a long talk about his hopes and dreams and he talked to me about his music. I had no idea that he could even sing! This talented singer/writer/musician was considering going to the classroom simply because that's what he thought I would want him to do. We talked about how I took a leap of faith and that I would support him in any decision that he made, but I wanted him to do what made him happy. He felt so relieved! Now he's pursuing his dreams as well.

　　I'm hoping that my story inspires you to stop being afraid. I hope you read this and recognizes your jars of oil sitting up on the shelf, waiting to become your blessing. I hope you read this and understand that God has already given you everything you need to be successful. Most importantly, I hope you read this and understand that above all, God loves you and will always be there to guide you along the way, no matter what path you are on.

So, let me ask you, what's your oil?

RESOURCES FOR SMALL BUSINESS OWNERS

Business Start-up Resources

Here's a list of resources that anyone can use to start, run, and grow a business. Most of them are FREE (my favorite word). Enjoy!

Element	Resources (Free = F; $ = Cost)
Business Plan	Score.org - Business Plan Template (F) https://www.score.org/resource/business-plan-template-startup-business
Grant Writing	How to get started with Grant Writing http://www.dummies.com/business/nonprofits/grants/grant-writing-for-dummies-cheat-sheet/
Cash flow	Score.org - Business Plan Template (F) https://www.score.org/resource/business-plan-template-startup-business

Funding sources	Small business funding info from US Black Chambers - http://www.pathwaystocapital.org/ Small Business Administration https://www.sba.gov/
Research competitors	Competitive Analysis Template (F) - http://blog.clientheartbeat.com/downloads/Competitive-Analysis-Template.pdf
Business name	Naming Your Business (F) - https://www.entrepreneur.com/article/76958
Business mailing address	USPS P.O. Boxes ($) - https://www.usps.com/manage/po-boxes.htm
Incorporate	Incorporate your business for free - https://www.rocketlawyer.com/incorporate-for-free.rl
Internal revenue ID number	Apply for your EIN (F) - https://www.irs.gov/businesses/small-businesses-self-employed/apply-for-an-employer-identification-number-ein-online

Legal Assistance	Low-cost legal documents - https://www.rocketlawyer.com/incorporate-for-free.rl
Register copyrights	Register for copyrights ($) - http://www.copyright.gov
Apply for patent	US Patent Office - https://www.uspto.gov/patent
Business License	Varies by State/County Virginia - https://www.virginia.gov/business/ North Carolina - https://edpnc.com/start-or-grow-a-business/start-a-business/license-permits/ DC - http://dcra.dc.gov/service/about-business-licensing
Business Insurance	Types of Business Insurance - https://www.sba.gov/managing-business/running-business/insurance/types-business-insurance

Accounting and accounting software	Quickbooks Online https://quickbooks.intuit.com/accountants/quickbooks-accountant/
Website	Create your own website! ($ - minimal) http://wix.com (my personal fav!)
Establish communications	Phone: - https://www.google.com/voice/?setup=1#setup/ - https://picup.com/ E-Mail: https://www.google.com/**gmail**/
Professional Headshots	Find a professional photographer in your area! https://www.thumbtack.com/
Social Media Marketing	Great advice article with resources - http://www.socialmediaexaminer.com/social-media-marketing-tips-pros/
Business cards and stationery and sales literature	Great resource for creating print material ($) - http://www.vistaprint.com/
Logo and literature design	Great resource for design work ($ - min.) - https://www.fiverr.com/

Online Directories **(IE. Yellow Pages)**	Free online directories guide - http://blog.signpost.com/free-online-directories-local-business-listings/
Execute your marketing plan	Score Marketing Webinar - https://www.score.org/event/marketing-qa-everything-you-want-know-about-small-biz-marketing
Grand Opening Event	Planning Your Grand Opening: http://fitsmallbusiness.com/grand-opening-ideas/

ABOUT THE AUTHOR

Maya Harris (Maya Lynn) may be an entrepreneur, but she will tell you that she is, and always will be, a teacher. She grew up in Windsor, CT and attended Virginia Union University, in Richmond, VA, where she obtained her B.A. in English. She became a teacher in 1998 and taught in the Hartford Public School System in Hartford, CT for five years before moving her family to Richmond, VA. In Richmond, she taught secondary English in Henrico County and Hanover Country for 12 years.

Maya worked as an educational consultant for 4 years before pursuing her dreams full-time as the CEO of LAMA Learning, an educational service company that focuses on creating alternative academic solutions for students and the community.

Maya L. Harris

Maya is the mother of two sons, Mandell and Bryce, who are her WHY for everything she does. She is the blessed daughter of Carl and Dorothy Harris.

PRAISE FOR *WHAT'S YOUR OIL?*

"I am so proud of Maya. Every woman needs to read this book. It's like having a personal road map to achieving your dreams and goals!"

Pasha Carter
TV Network Owner, Direct Sales TV Network
Speaker and Direct Sales Professional
www.PashaCarter.com

༄༄༄༄༄

"Maya has done a skillful and eloquent job of weaving her life experience in between and throughout the story of the unnamed widow in the Bible. Whether you are a person of faith or not, you will find yourself asking "What's Your Oil?". More importantly, Maya challenges all of us to look at perceived lack or scarcity in our lives and flip it on its side to change the direction of our dreams, businesses, and pursuits. This resourceful book will guide you through this process, step by step!"

Sharvette Mitchell
Coach, Web Designer and Talk Radio Host
"Enabling female entrepreneurs to build their platform so they generate revenue."
www.SharvetteMitchell.com

༄༄༄༄༄

"You don't know the cost of Maya's oil, but one thing is certain …she has always demonstrated her faith and trust in the Lord! The gifted teacher within her has provided the reader with the lessons learned and the knowledge to pass the test."

Yolanda Reed
President and CEO, Credential America
www.CredentialAmerica.com

www.ingramcontent.com/pod-product-compliance
Lightning Source LLC
LaVergne TN
LVHW041635070426
835507LV00008B/640